FOOD LOVERS

DESSERT

RECIPES SELECTED BY ALEKSANDRA MALYSKA

Trans
Atlantic
Press

All recipes serve four people, unless otherwise indicated.

For best results when cooking the recipes in this book, buy fresh ingredients and follow the instructions carefully. Make sure that everything is properly cooked through before serving and note that as a general rule vulnerable groups such as the very young, elderly people, pregnant women and convalescents should avoid dishes that contain raw eggs.

For all recipes, quantities are given in standard U.S. cups and imperial measures, followed by the metric equivalent. Follow one set or the other, but not a mixture of both because conversions may not be exact. Standard spoon and cup measurements are level and are based on the following:

1 tsp. = 5 ml, 1 tbsp. = 15 ml, 1 cup = 250 ml / 8 fl oz.

Note that Australian standard tablespoons are 20 ml, so Australian readers should use 3 tsp. in place of 1 tbsp. when measuring small quantities.

The electric oven temperatures in this book are given for conventional ovens with top and bottom heat. When using a fan oven, the temperature should be decreased by about 20–40°F / 10–20°C – check the oven manufacturer's instruction book for further guidance. The cooking times given should be used as a guideline.

CONTENTS

RHUBARB AND APPLE TART

Ingredients

4 apples

11 oz / 300 g rhubarb

1–2 tbsp. / 15–25 g butter

1 tbsp. sugar

7 oz / 200 g puff pastry, defrosted if frozen

For the caramel

2 fl oz / 50 ml water

½ cup / 100 g sugar

2 tbsp. / 25 g butter

8 tbsp. vanilla ice cream, to serve

Method

Prep and cook time: 1 hour 30 min.

1 Preheat the oven to 190°C (375°F/Gas Mark 5). For the caramel, heat the water and sugar in a saucepan and boil until golden brown. Remove immediately from the heat and stir in the butter. Pour immediately into a 6–8 inch (15–20 cm) tart pan (tin).

2 For the filling, peel, quarter and core the apples, and then slice into wedges. Cut the rhubarb into 1 inch (3 cm) pieces. Tightly pack the fruit alternatively into the tart pan. Melt the butter and brush over the fruit and then sprinkle the sugar over the top.

3 Bake in the oven for 35–40 minutes. Meanwhile, roll out the pastry very thinly to a circle measuring about 8 inch (20 cm) in diameter. Remove the tart from the oven and place the puff pastry over the top. Press the sides in with a spoon handle.

4 Return to the oven and bake for a further 30 minutes until golden brown. Remove from the oven and leave to cool slightly then turn out on to a serving plate. Serve with a few scoops of vanilla ice cream.

COFFEE MOUSSE

Ingredients

5 oz / 150 g milk chocolate, at least 30% cocoa solids

2 leaves gelatin (gelatine)

4 tbsp. instant coffee powder

1½ cups / 300 ml whipping cream

2 eggs

1½ tbsp. coffee liqueur

Pinch of salt

2½ tbsp. sugar

Whipped cream, to serve

Cocoa powder, to decorate

Method

Prep and cook time: 40 min. plus 4 hours chilling

1 Break up the chocolate and melt in a bowl standing over a pan of simmering water. Soak the gelatin (gelatine) in cold water. Mix the coffee powder with a scant ½ cup (100 ml) of the cream.

2 Separate 1 egg and beat the egg yolk and the whole egg with the coffee cream in a bowl standing over a pan of simmering water, until thick and creamy. Squeeze out the gelatin and stir into the mixture until dissolved. Remove the bowl from the heat and add the chocolate and coffee liqueur. Stir until cold.

3 Whisk the egg white with a pinch of salt until stiff, trickling in the sugar at the same time. Whisk the remaining cream until stiff and fold both into the coffee mixture.

4 Divide the mousse between 4 dishes and chill in the refrigerator for at least 4 hours.

5 To serve, add a topping of whipped cream and dust with cocoa powder to decorate.

PEAR AND HAZELNUT TART

Ingredients

2 oz / 50 g dark chocolate,
at least 70% cocoa solids

¼ cup / 50 ml espresso coffee

3 eggs

½ cup / 100 g sugar

Seeds from 1 vanilla bean (pod)

1 cup / 100 g ground hazelnuts

1 tsp. baking powder

2 tbsp. all-purpose (plain) flour

5–6 peeled, poached pears

2 oz /50 g dark chocolate, at least
70% cocoa solids, to decorate

For the pastry

2 cups / 200 g all-purpose (plain) flour

Heaped ½ cup / 60 g confectioners'
(icing) sugar

Pinch of salt

½ cup /100 g butter

Dried peas or beans, for baking blind

Method

Prep and cook time: 1 hour 30 min. plus 1 hour chilling

1 To make the pastry, put the flour, confectioners' (icing) sugar and salt in a bowl. Chop the butter into small pieces, add to the flour and using a knife or your fingertips, rub in until the mixture resembles coarse breadcrumbs. Combine all ingredients and knead to form a soft dough. Wrap in plastic wrap (clingfilm) and chill in the refrigerator for 1 hour.

2 Preheat the oven to 180°C (375°F/Gas Mark 5). Roll out the pastry on a lightly floured surface and use to line a 10 inch (25 cm) tart pan (tin), allowing 2 inch (5 cm) to hang over the edge. Place a sheet of parchment paper on the pastry and put the dried beans on top. Bake in the oven for about 15 minutes, until set. Remove the baking parchment and dried beans and leave to cool.

3 To make the filling, melt the chocolate in the espresso. Beat the eggs and sugar together until light and creamy. Stir in the vanilla seeds and the espresso chocolate. Mix the ground hazelnuts, baking powder and flour together in a bowl, and then fold into the eggs.

4 Drain and cut the pears in half, and arrange them in the pastry case. Pour the filling on top and smooth. Bake in the oven for about 40 minutes. Test with a toothpick (cocktail stick) to see if the cake is cooked. If the cake is becoming too brown, cover with a piece of foil. Remove from the oven, leave to cool, and then carefully remove the tart from the pan.

5 To decorate, melt the chocolate in a bowl, standing over a saucepan of simmering water, and then drizzle thin lines over the top of the tart in a criss-cross pattern.

POACHED RED WINE PEARS

Ingredients

1 unwaxed lemon

¾ cup / 150 g sugar

1 cinnamon stick

3 cups / 750 ml red wine

4 small-medium cooking pears

8 walnut halves

Method

Prep and cook time: 30 min

1 Slice the lemon and put in a saucepan with the sugar, cinnamon stick and red wine. Bring to a boil then simmer gently for about 10 minutes.

2 Peel the pears, leaving the stalks on. Remove the cinnamon stick and lemon slices from the red wine. Stand the pears upright in a deep saucepan and pour in the wine, making sure that it covers the pears. Cover the pan and poach the pears over a low heat for about 10 minutes.

3 Take the pears out of the poaching liquid and stand on individual serving plates.

4 Boil the red wine until reduced to a syrupy consistency. Add the walnuts and mix into the sauce. Pour the hot red wine sauce over the pears and leave until cold before serving.

LEMON MOUSSE WITH ALMONDS

Ingredients

Grated peel 1 lemon

1 cup / 225 ml freshly squeezed lemon juice

1 cup / 225 ml white wine

¾ cup / 150 g sugar

¼ cup / 40 g cornstarch (cornflour)

2 egg yolks

3 egg whites

4 unwaxed lemons

2/3 cup / 50 g toasted chopped almonds

Cookies, to serve

Mint leaves, to decorate

Method

Prep and cook time: 20 min plus 3 hours chilling

1 Put the lemon peel, juice, ½ cup (125 ml) of the wine and ½ cup (100 g) of the sugar into a saucepan.

2 Mix the cornstarch with the egg yolks and the remaining wine. Stir the mixture into the pan and bring to a boil, stirring all the time.

3 Whisk the egg whites until they form stiff peaks, gradually adding the remaining sugar. Stir into the hot mixture, and then transfer to a bowl. Leave to cool and then chill in the refrigerator for at least 3 hours.

4 Cut a lid off each lemon and hollow out the fruit. Fill the lemons with the chilled mousse and sprinkle with toasted almonds. Serve with cookies of your choice.

CRÈME BRÛLÉE

Ingredients

Scant 1 cup / 200 ml milk

Scant 1 cup / 200 ml whipping cream

1 vanilla bean (pod)

2 eggs

2 egg yolks

¼ cup / 50 g sugar

Sugar, for sprinkling on top

Method

Prep and cook time: 45 min. plus 3-4 hours chilling

1 Preheat the oven to 200°C (400°F/Gas Mark 6). Put the milk and cream in a saucepan. Slit the vanilla bean (pod) in half lengthways, scrape out the seeds and add both seeds and bean to the milk and bring to a boil.

2 Beat the eggs and egg yolks with the sugar until creamy, but not frothy, and gradually stir in the hot milk.

3 Strain the mixture into individual dishes, put in a roasting pan (tin) and pour in enough hot water to come two-thirds of the way up the dishes. Cook in the oven, uncovered, for 20–25 minutes, until set.

4 Remove from the pan and leave to cool for 1 hour then chill in the refrigerator for 2–3 hours.

5 Before serving, sprinkle sugar on top to lightly cover and put under a hot broiler (grill) until the surface is caramelized. Alternatively, caramelize the top with a cook's blowtorch.

GRANITA DI CAFFÈ

Ingredients

Scant ½ cup / 80 g sugar

½ cup / 125 ml water

1¼ cups / 350 ml strong, hot espresso or coffee

1 vanilla bean (pod)

Scant ½ cup / 100 ml whipping cream

4 tsp. espresso

Amaretti cookies, to serve

Method

Prep and cook time: 3 hours

1 Put 1/3 cup (70 g) of the sugar and the water in a saucepan and mix well together. Bring to a boil and boil vigorously for 1 minute. Add the espresso or coffee. Slit the vanilla bean (pod) in half lengthways, scrape out the seeds and add both seeds and bean to the coffee syrup. Leave to cool.

2 Strain the mixture through a sieve into a shallow, freezer-proof container and put into the freezer for 2 hours, stirring vigorously with a fork every 30 minutes to prevent any large ice crystals from forming. Stir once more at the end of the 2 hours.

3 Whisk the cream with the remaining sugar and the espresso until semi-stiff.

4 Spoon the granita into 4 glasses, add a small spoonful of cream and serve with amaretti cookies.

PORTUGUESE RICE WITH CINNAMON

Ingredients

4 cups / 1 litre milk

2 tsp. grated lemon peel

Scant ½ cup / 100 g pudding (short-grain) rice

1/3 cup / 70 g sugar

5 eggs

Cinnamon, to decorate

Method

Prep and cook time: 1 hour plus 2–3 hours chilling

1 Take 4 tablespoons of the milk and set aside. Put the remaining milk in a saucepan with the lemon peel and bring to a boil. Add the rice and sugar, cover, and cook very gently over a low heat for about 40 minutes until the rice is swollen and soft.

2 Separate the eggs. Whisk the egg whites until stiff. Whisk the egg yolks with the reserved milk and add to the rice. Reheat, but do not let it boil again.

3 Remove from the heat and fold in the whisked egg whites. Spoon into bowls, decorate with cinnamon and chill well in the refrigerator before serving.

CHOCOLATE PUDDINGS

Ingredients

¼ cup / 60 g butter, plus extra for greasing

½ cup / 100 g sugar, plus extra for sprinkling

½ cup / 50 g walnuts

½ cup / 125 ml milk

1 vanilla bean (pod)

2 oz / 50 g dark chocolate, at least 64% cocoa solids

½ cup / 60 g all-purpose (plain) flour

4 eggs

Confectioners' (icing) sugar, for dusting

A little whipped cream

Method

Prep and cook time: 1 hour

1 Preheat the oven to 180°C (350°F/Gas Mark 4). Grease 4 ovenproof molds and sprinkle with a little of the sugar. Put the walnuts in a food processor and grind finely. Put the milk and the vanilla bean (pod) in a saucepan, bring to a boil then set aside. Break the chocolate into a bowl and melt, standing over a pan of simmering water.

2 Melt the butter in a pan, stir in the flour and cook, without browning, until the paste is smooth. Remove the vanilla bean from the milk and slowly stir the hot milk into the pan, stirring all the time. Simmer gently for about 10 minutes, stirring occasionally. Transfer the mixture to a bowl and leave to cool slightly.

3 Separate the eggs and gradually stir 1 egg white and the egg yolks into the cooled mixture. Stir in the melted chocolate and the nuts. Whisk the remaining egg whites with the sugar until stiff and stir a quarter into the mixture with a whisk. Fold the rest in carefully with a metal spoon.

4 Put the batter into the prepared molds, filling them three-quarters full. Put in a roasting pan (tin) and pour in enough hot water to come two-thirds of the way up the molds. Bake in the oven for 25–30 minutes.

5 Turn out of the molds, dust with a little confectioners' (icing) sugar and top with whipped cream. Serve at once.

QUARK AND APRICOT STRUDEL

Ingredients

Scant 1 cup / 85 g whole grain wheat

1 cup plus 2 tbsp / 250 ml milk

Pinch of salt

Scant ½ cup / 100 g butter, plus extra
for greasing

4 eggs

3 cups / 750 g quark (curd) cheese

½ tsp. cinnamon

Scant ½ cup / 100 g sugar

Grated peel and juice 1 untreated
lemon

14 oz / 400 g apricots

Flour, for dusting

Confectioners' (icing) sugar, for dusting

For the pastry

2½ cups / 250 g all-purpose
(plain) flour

1 egg

Pinch of salt

2 tbsp. vegetable oil

½ cup / 100 ml lukewarm water

Method

Prep and cook time: 1 hour 20 min. plus 30 min resting

1 Put the wheat, milk and salt in a saucepan, bring to
the boil then simmer for 8–10 minutes, or according to
the instructions on the packet. Drain and leave to cool.

2 Meanwhile, make the pastry. Put all ingredients
in a bowl and mix together. Knead until the dough is
smooth, and then form a ball, cover with plastic wrap
(clingfilm) and leave to rest for about 30 minutes.

3 Preheat the oven to 200°C (400°F/Gas Mark 6).
Grease a baking sheet. Separate the eggs. Put the quark,
cinnamon, sugar, egg yolks, lemon juice and peel in a
bowl and mix together. Add the wheat. Whisk the egg
whites until beginning to hold their shape and then
carefully fold into the quark mixture. Remove the stones
from the apricots and cut the flesh into thin slices.

4 Melt the butter and set aside. Roll out the strudel
pastry very thinly on a floured kitchen towel (tea towel),
then pull and stretch until wafer-thin. Brush the pastry
with a little melted butter. Spread the filling over the
pastry, and then scatter the apricots over the top.

5 Use the kitchen towel to carefully roll the sides of
the strudel towards the middle. Place the strudel on the
prepared baking sheet and brush with the melted butter.
Bake in the oven for about 45 minutes. Cut into slices, dust
with confectioners' (icing) sugar and serve.

CHEESECAKES WITH BERRIES

Ingredients

2 cups / 500 g quark (curd) cheese

2/3 cup / 125 g sugar

1/4 cup / 40 g cornstarch (cornflour)

4 eggs

2 tsp. grated lemon peel

Scant 1 cup / 200 ml whipping cream

2 cups / 250 g raspberries

2 cups / 250 g strawberries

2 tbsp. sugar

2 tbsp. water

For the pastry

1 3/4 cups / 200 g all-purpose (plain) flour

2 tsp. cocoa powder

Pinch of salt

2 tbsp. sugar

Scant 1/2 cup / 100 g cold butter

1 egg

About 1/4 cup / 50 ml lukewarm water

Method

Prep and cook time: 1 hour 45 min.

1 To make the pastry, put the flour in a heap on a work surface, mix with the cocoa, salt and sugar and make a well in the middle. Cut the cold butter into small pieces and scatter around the well. Break the egg into the middle, add the water and chop all the ingredients with a knife until they resemble breadcrumbs. Quickly combine to a dough with your hands, form into a ball, wrap in plastic wrap (clingfilm) and chill in the refrigerator for about 30 minutes.

2 Preheat the oven to 180°C (350°F/Gas Mark 4). Roll out the pastry between 2 sheets of baking parchment and cut out 8 circles to fit four 4 inch (10 cm) individual molds, using either the rim of one of the molds or a 4 inch (10 cm) cutter. Line the bases of the greased molds with the pastry circles.

3 For the filling, mix the quark with the sugar, cornstarch (cornflour), eggs and grated lemon peel. Whisk the cream until stiff and fold in. Fill the molds with the mixture and smooth the top.

4 Bake in the oven for about 40 minutes. (Test to see if they are cooked by inserting a wooden cocktail stick.) When cooked, leave in the oven for a further 10 minutes, with the oven switched off and the door open a crack. Remove from the oven and leave to cool.

5 To serve, remove the cheesecakes from the molds and put on serving plates. Put a third of each of the raspberries and strawberries in a small saucepan. Add the sugar and water and bring to a boil. Push the sauce through a sieve. Drizzle the cheesecakes with the fruit sauce and top with the remaining fresh fruit.

Serves 8

HERB TEA WITH LEMON SORBET

Ingredients

Handful of mint

4 cups / 1 litre water, plus 5 tbsp.

¾ cup / 150 g sugar

½ cup / 125 ml lemon juice

½ cup / 125 ml lime juice

Scant ½ cup / 100 ml white wine

1 egg white

Method

Prep and cook time: 20 min. plus 4 hours freezing

1 Put the mint, reserving a little to decorate, and the 4 cups (1 litre) water in a saucepan and bring to a boil. Remove from the heat and leave to stand for 5–10 minutes, depending on taste. Strain and chill in the refrigerator.

2 Meanwhile, put the sugar into a pan with the 5 tablespoons water. Bring to the boil and boil until syrupy. Strain the lemon and lime juice into the syrup and add the wine.

3 Whisk the egg white until stiff and fold into the mixture. Turn into a shallow freezer-proof container and put into the freezer for 4 hours, stirring vigorously with a fork every hour to prevent any large ice crystals from forming. Stir once more at the end of the 4 hours.

4 To serve, put scoops of sorbet into serving glasses and fill up with the ice-cold mint tea. Serve decorated with the reserved mint, torn into shreds.

TIRAMISU

Ingredients

2½ oz / 60 g dark chocolate, at least 70% cocoa solids

Scant ½ cup / 100 g quark (curd) cheese

2/3 cup / 150 g mascarpone cheese

¼ cup / 30 g confectioners' (icing) sugar

2/3 cup / 150 ml whipping cream

1 cup / 250 ml espresso coffee

3 tbsp Amaretto

8 lady finger cookies

Cocoa powder, for dusting

Method

Prep and cook time: 30 min. plus 1 hour chilling

1 Break the chocolate into a bowl and melt, standing over a saucepan of simmering water. Leave to cool slightly.

2 Put the quark, mascarpone and confectioners' (icing) sugar in a bowl and mix together. Whisk the cream until stiff and fold into the mascarpone mixture.

3 Mix the espresso with the Amaretto and break the lady finger cookies into pieces. Divide a third of the lady fingers between 4 glasses and soak with a third of the espresso and Amaretto. Cover with a third of the cream and pour over half of the melted chocolate. Add two more layers of ingredients in the same order, ending with cream.

4 Put in the refrigerator for at least 1 hour to chill. Serve dusted with cocoa powder.

CHOCOLATE ROULADE WITH STRAWBERRIES

Ingredients

Scant 1 cup / 100 g all-purpose (plain) flour

1 tsp. baking powder

4 tbsp. cocoa powder

Pinch of salt

4 eggs

4 tbsp. cold water

¾ cup / 150 g sugar

Sugar, for sprinkling

For the filling

3 cups / 400 g strawberries

½ cup / 100 g sugar

Scant 1 cup / 200 ml heavy (double) cream

1 tsp. vanilla extract

Scant 1 cup / 200 g mascarpone cheese

Confectioners' (icing) sugar, for dusting

Mint leaves, for decorating

Method

Prep and cook time: 1 hour plus 3 hours chilling

1 Preheat the oven to 200°C (400°F/Gas Mark 6). Line a jelly roll pan (Swiss roll tin) with baking parchment. To make the sponge, put the flour, baking powder, cocoa and salt in a bowl and mix together. Separate the eggs.

2 Whisk the egg whites with the water until stiff, trickling in the sugar. Fold in the egg yolks. Sift the flour mixture over and fold in carefully. Spread the batter in the prepared pan and bake in the oven for 10-15 minutes.

3 Turn out on to a tea towel sprinkled with sugar and pull off the baking parchment. Roll up, cover and leave to cool.

4 For the filling, quarter the strawberries. Mix with ¼ cup (50 g) of the sugar. Whisk the cream with the vanilla extract and ¼ cup (50 g) sugar until stiff. Fold in the mascarpone cheese.

5 Unroll the sponge and spread with the cream. Scatter the strawberries over the cream and roll up again with the help of the tea towel. Chill in the refrigerator for at least 3 hours. Serve sprinkled with confectioners' (icing) sugar and decorate with mint leaves.

HONEY COFFEE CREAMS WITH HONEY SWEETS

Ingredients

¼ cup / 50 g sugar

4 tbsp. water

1 tbsp. instant coffee powder

2 eggs

2 egg yolks

¼ cup / 100 g honey

½ cup / 125 ml milk

1¼ cups / 275 ml whipping cream

4 honey sweets

Method

Prep and cook time: 1 hour 15 plus 2 hours chilling

1 Preheat the oven to 180°C (350°F/Gas Mark 4). Put the sugar and water in a saucepan and heat until lightly caramelized. Remove from the heat and leave to cool slightly.

2 Stir the coffee into the caramel and divide between 4 ovenproof glasses.

3 Put the eggs, egg yolks and honey in a bowl and mix together until slightly creamy. Put the milk and cream in a saucepan, bring to a boil, and then stir into the egg mixture. Strain through a sieve and pour on to the coffee caramel.

4 Put the filled glasses in a roasting pan (tin) and pour in enough hot water to come three-quarters of the way up the glasses. Cook in the oven for 35–40 minutes.

5 Remove from the oven, leave to cool and chill in the refrigerator for at least 2 hours. Roughly crush the honey sweets and scatter on top of the honey creams before serving.

CHOCOLATE AND ALMOND CAKE

Ingredients

8 eggs

1¼ cups / 200 g ground almonds

Heaped 2 cups / 500 g sugar

1 cup / 225 g butter

1¼ oz / 35 g cornstarch (cornflour)

2 oz / 50 g dark chocolate, at least 70% cocoa solids

For the frosting

5 oz / 140 g dark chocolate, at least 70% cocoa solids

5 tbsp. whipping cream

Method

Prep and cook time: 1 h 45 min

1 Preheat the oven to 200°C (400°F/Gas Mark 6). Line a 10 in (25 cm) spring-form pan (tin) with parchment paper. Separate the eggs. Whisk half of the egg whites until stiff. Fold half of the ground almonds and a heaped ½ cup (125 g) of the sugar into the egg whites, a little at a time. Pour the batter into the prepared pan (tin). Bake in the oven for 15–20 minutes. Repeat this process for the second cake, using the remaining ground almonds and a heaped ½ cup (125 g) of the sugar.

2 Put the butter in a bowl and melt, standing over a saucepan of hot water. Do not allow it to become too hot. Stir in the remaining heaped 1 cup (250 g) sugar, the cornstarch (cornflour) and egg yolks. Leave to cool slightly. Break the chocolate into a bowl and melt, standing over a saucepan of hot water. Leave to cool slightly. Stir the chocolate into the butter cream and mix until soft and creamy.

3 Spoon about a third of the chocolate cream on to an almond cake. Place the second cake on the top. Spoon the remaining chocolate cream over the top.

4 For the frosting, break the chocolate into a bowl. Add the cream and melt over a pan of hot water. Leave to cool, and then stir until creamy and spread over the chocolate almond cake.

CHOCOLATE SOUFFLÉ

Ingredients

Butter, for greasing

Scant ½ cup / 100 g sugar, plus extra for sprinkling

6 oz / 175 g dark chocolate, at least 65% cocoa solids

5 tbsp. milk

2 tsp. cocoa powder

5 eggs

2 tsp. all-purpose (plain) flour

Confectioners' (icing) sugar, for dusting

Method

Prep and cook time: 1 hour 20 min.

1 Preheat the oven to 180°C (350°F/Gas Mark 4). Put a deep baking pan (tin), half-filled with water, on the lowest shelf of the oven. Grease a soufflé dish with butter and sprinkle with sugar. Place in the refrigerator.

2 Break up the chocolate. Put the milk, cocoa powder and half of the sugar in a saucepan and heat until warm. Remove from the heat, add the chocolate and stir until melted.

3 Separate the eggs. Stir the egg yolks and the flour into the chocolate mixture. Whisk the egg whites and the remaining sugar together until stiff. Fold carefully into the chocolate mixture.

4 Turn the mixture into the prepared soufflé dish and place in the oven in the baking pan. Bake for about 50 minutes. The middle of the soufflé should be soft and runny. Dust with confectioners' (icing) sugar and serve immediately.

RASPBERRY-PEACH CRISP

Ingredients

Oil, for greasing

2/3 cup / 50 g flaked almonds

2 tbsp. finely chopped hazelnuts

Scant 1/2 cup / 100 ml honey

1 tbsp. / 15 g butter

3–4 heaped tbsp. fine rolled oats

4–5 peaches

2 1/2 cups / 300 g raspberries

Juice of 1 lemon

1–2 tbsp. sugar

1 tsp. vanilla extract

Method

Prep and cook time: 40 min

1 Preheat the oven to 200°C (400°F/Gas Mark 6). Grease a baking sheet and line another baking sheet with baking parchment. Spread the almonds and hazelnuts out on the lined baking sheet and toast in the oven for 2–3 minutes.

2 Meanwhile, put the honey and butter into a small saucepan and bring to a boil, stirring occasionally. Boil for 5–7 minutes. Add the nuts and rolled oats to the caramelized honey, mix well and spread on the greased baking sheet. Leave to set.

3 Cut the peaches in half, remove the stones and cut the flesh into bite-size pieces. Heat the raspberries in a saucepan with the lemon juice. Stir in the sugar and vanilla extract.

4 Push half of the raspberries through a sieve to form a purée. Mix with the peaches and the remaining raspberries and divide between serving glasses.

5 Break up the set caramel and chop roughly in a food processor. Scatter over the raspberry and peach mixture and serve.

BREAD PUDDING WITH RHUBARB

Ingredients

Butter, for greasing

1 stick rhubarb

¼ cup / 50 ml white wine

4 tbsp. sugar

6 slices white bread

Scant 1 cup / 200 ml whipping cream

4 eggs

Seeds from a vanilla bean (pod)

Large pinch of cinnamon

Confectioners' (icing) sugar, for dusting

Method

Prep and cook time: 45 min

1 Preheat the oven to 180°C (350°F/Gas Mark 4). Butter an ovenproof dish. Cut the rhubarb into thin strips.

2 Put the white wine in a saucepan, bring to a boil, add the rhubarb and 2 tablespoons of the sugar and simmer for about 10 minutes.

3 Arrange the bread neatly in the prepared dish, overlapping the slices. Put the cream, eggs, vanilla seeds, cinnamon and the remaining 2 tablespoons of sugar in a bowl and whisk together. Pour over the bread.

4 Place the stewed rhubarb over the top of the dish and bake in the oven for about 20 minutes, until golden brown. Dust with confectioners' (icing) sugar before serving.

CRÈME CARAMEL WITH BERRIES

Ingredients

Scant 1 cup / 175 g sugar

Scant ½ cup / 100 ml milk

2 eggs

2 egg yolks

1 cup / 250 ml whipping cream

2 cups / 200 g mixed berries, of your choice

Method

Prep and cook time: 40 min. plus 3 hours chilling

1 Preheat the oven to 170°C (325°F/Gas Mark 3). Put a deep baking pan (tin), three-quarters filled with boiling water, in the oven.

2 Put $1/3$ cup (70 g) sugar in a heavy-based saucepan and heat until lightly caramelized. Put 1 tablespoon of the caramel into 4 shallow ovenproof dishes, measuring 4–5 inch (10-13 cm) in diameter.

3 Warm the milk in a pan. Put the eggs, egg yolks, remaining sugar, cream and warm milk in a bowl and whisk together. Strain through a sieve and pour on to the caramel in the dishes.

4 Place the filled dishes in the pan and cook in the oven for about 30 minutes. Test to see if they are cooked by inserting a toothpick (cocktail stick) in the centre. Leave to cool, and then chill in the refrigerator for at least 3 hours.

5 To serve, briefly dip the dishes in hot water, run the tip of a knife around the rim and turn out on to dessert plates. Serve with fresh berries of your choice.

LEMON CUSTARD PARFAITS

Ingredients

1 cup / 250 ml milk

1 cup / 250 ml whipping cream

¼ cup / 75 g honey (runny or set)

4 tbsp. limoncello (lemon liqueur)

5 egg yolks

Grated zest 2 unwaxed lemons

Confectioners' (icing) sugar, for dusting

4 strawberries

Method

Prep and cook time: 30 min plus chilling time 1 h

1 Put the milk, cream and limoncello in a saucepan, mix together and bring to a boil. Remove from the heat.

2 Put the egg yolks and honey in a bowl and beat until creamy. Slowly pour the warm milk into the egg yolk mixture in a thin stream, stirring all the time. Return to the pan and beat over a very low heat until the custard thickens. Do not let it boil.

3 Stir in the lemon zest, reserving a little for decoration, and leave to cool to lukewarm, stirring occasionally.

4 Divide about a third of the custard between 4 serving glasses, put a strawberry into each glass and fill up with the remaining custard. Dust with a little confectioners' (icing) sugar and chill in the refrigerator for at least 1 hour. Serve decorated with the reserved lemon zest.

CREPES SUZETTE

Ingredients

2 eggs

Scant 1 cup / 250 ml milk

1¼ cups / 125 g all-purpose (plain) flour

1 tbsp. sugar

Butter, for frying

For the sauce

4 unwaxed oranges

4 tbsp. sugar

3 tbsp. / 40 g butter

5 tbsp. Grand Marnier

Method

Prep and cook time: 45 min. plus 20 min. standing

1 To make the pancakes, beat the eggs, milk, flour and sugar to a smooth batter and leave to stand for 20 minutes.

2 To make the sauce, cut thin strands of zest from 2 of the oranges. Peel all the oranges using a sharp knife, removing all the white pith and skin. Cut down between the segments and remove the segments, catching the juice as you work into a bowl. Squeeze any remaining juice out of the oranges into the bowl.

3 Heat the sugar and butter in a skillet (frying pan) until caramelized. Stir in the orange juice. Simmer until a smooth sauce is formed, and then add the orange zest and segments. Remove from the heat.

4 Heat a little butter in another skillet and make 8 thin crêpes, one after the other. Fold each into a triangle. Place the crêpes in the orange sauce and warm briefly.

5 Add the Grand Marnier and flambé. Serve on warmed plates with the orange sauce.

Published by Transatlantic Press

First published in 2010

Transatlantic Press
38 Copthorne Road, Croxley Green, Hertfordshire WD3 4AQ

© Transatlantic Press

Images and Recipes by StockFood © The Food Image Agency

Recipes selected by Aleksandra Malyska, StockFood

A catalogue record for this book is available from the British Library.

ISBN 978-1-908533-63-0

Printed in China